CW00695295

FORT WORTH, TEXAS

A PHOTOGRAPHIC PORTRAIT

PHOTOGRAPHY BY

PETER A. CALVIN

Copyright © 2007 by
Twin Lights Publishers, Inc.

All rights reserved. No part of this book may be
reproduced in any form without written permission
of the copyright owners. All images in this book have
been reproduced with the knowledge and prior con-
sent of the artists concerned and no responsibility is
accepted by producer, publisher, or printer for any
infringement of copyright or otherwise, arising from
the contents of this publication. Every effort has been
made to ensure that credits accurately comply with
information supplied.

First published in the United States of America by:

Twin Lights Publishers, Inc.
8 Hale Street
Rockport, Massachusetts 01966
Telephone: (978) 546-7398
http://www.twinlightspub.com

ISBN: 1-885435-82-7
ISBN: 978-1-885435-82-8

10 9 8 7 6 5 4 3 2 1

Leather and Line (*opposite*)

Through the eyes of a photographer, horse tack takes
on certain qualities of beauty and grace.

(*jacket front*)

Beaumont Ranch at Grandview

(*jacket back*)

Flying Man with Briefcase in Burnett Park

This book is dedicated to my wife, Ana Rosa, whose
love and support has made my work on this project,
and all others, possible, and to our son, Peter Jose,
whose contributions of hard work and good company as
my assistant have been invaluable.

Editorial researched and written by:
Francesca and Duncan Yates
www.freelancewriters.com

Book design by:
SYP Design & Production, Inc.
www.sypdesign.com

Printed in China

INTRODUCTION

Where the West Begins

You can never take the "Wild West" out of Fort Worth, even though it is one of the most cultured and cosmopolitan cities in America.

Fort Worth was a new military post in 1849, one of ten along the Trinity River. By 1853, the military moved further west, and the first settlers took over Fort Worth. Soon after the Civil War, this "Wild West" town got an economic shot in the arm as cattle drovers started moving Texas longhorns right through Fort Worth on their way to beef markets in Kansas. Fort Worth quickly became the last important stop on the famous Chisholm Trail, the frontier's version of an interstate highway.

When the railroad came to town years later, the city was on its way to becoming the second largest livestock market in the country. When oil was struck in nearby Spindletop in 1901, life got even better.

Cowboys and Culture

Downtown Fort Worth has been recharged and revitalized by Sundance Square, a world-class cultural and entertainment center, as well as the Historic Stockyards District, offering everything from boutiques and championship rodeos to cattle drives, and Billy Bob's, the largest "honky-tonk" in the world.

In this special photographic portrait, photographer Peter A. Calvin has captured the many moods of this vibrant city where one minute, you are admiring a Picasso and the next, you're at the rodeo. Page after page of evocative images will show you the heart and soul of this great American city.

Beaumont Ranch

Long-horn steer find relief from the blazing Texas sun under a lone, shady tree, while a llama enjoys the heat, at Beaumont Ranch. The ranch is one of the stops along the historic Chisholm Trail.

Flying Man with Briefcase

American sculptor Jonathan Borofsky is
known for his larger-than-life interpreta-
tions of the ordinary, including this 50-foot
structure in Fort Worth's Burnett Park.
Flying Man with Briefcase focuses on man
as a corporate slave.

Fort Worth Public Market

Stained glass and ornate details adorn the entrance tower of this architecturally rich building. The Public Market was Fort Worth's original farmers market from 1930–1941, and is currently undergoing renovation.

The Tower (*opposite*)

After a tornado heavily damaged the original thirty-five-story Bank One Tower, it was extensively renovated and transformed into luxury condominiums and penthouses, with retail and commercial space on the lower floors, and renamed "The Tower".

Tile Style (*above*)

Fort Worth reflects its Spanish heritage in the architecture of many of its modern buildings. In the 1920's and '30's, Spanish Colonial Revival was a very popular style with its extensive use of colorful, ceramic tiles.

Renaissance Revival (*left, right, and opposite*)

An historic landmark, the Flatiron Building was inspired by the 1902 Flatiron Building in New York City. Ironically, William Jenkins Worth, the man for whom Fort Worth is named, is buried at the New York building's base. Elaborately detailed inside and out, the Flatiron personifies Renaissance Revival architecture with its fretwork, gargoyles, and pediments. This city's first skyscraper was heavily criticized with fears that it would cast a shadow over Fort Worth's entire downtown area. Fears long sinced dispelled, the building is currently being renovated for residential use.

Fort Worth Convention Center *(top and bottom)*

Newly expanded and updated, the spacious Fort Worth Convention Center covers fourteen blocks downtown. In addition to meetings, conferences and conventions, the center's multi-purpose arena is home to Fort Worth Brahmas ice hockey team and the Worth Flyers basketball team in the NBA Development League. The 11,200-seat facility also hosts concerts and other notable events.

Sundance Square *(opposite)*

It was called *Hell's Half Acre* when the notorious Butch Cassidy and the Sundance Kid frequented the area. Today, its 21st-century entertainment, shopping, dining, art galleries and museums coincide amidst historic, 19th-century buildings.

Amon Carter Museum Statuary

The Amon Carter Museum holds one of the country's leading collections of American art, from the 1820's through 20th-century Modernists and 21st-century Contemporary painters, sculptors and photographers. Especially noteworthy are over one-hundred paintings and sculptures depicting the old West by Frederick Remington and Charles M. Russell, the most comprehensive collection of these artists' famous works in the world.

Postmodern Extraordinaire (*top*)

Born in a one-room log cabin, Amon Carter became a successful businessman and Fort Worth's most avid promoter and philanthropist. A lover of American art, he funded the museum to make fine art accessible to everyone.

American Art Treasures (*bottom*)

Opened in 1961, the art museum was designed by noted architect Philip Johnson, pioneer of the Postmodernist movement. This bold glass and steel style defined American skylines for fifty years, emphasizing form and function.

Quiet Courtyard

Ground-breaking ceremonies for the First Methodist Church's new sanctuary were held on October 29, 1929, the infamous day of the Stock Market crash. A testimony to faith and determination, the church opened its doors one year later.

Historic First Methodist Church

Once a one-room, wooden building in 1874, the First United Methodist Church has steadily grown in size and stature in the Fort Worth community. Since 1930, several additions have accommodated its ever-increasing congregation.

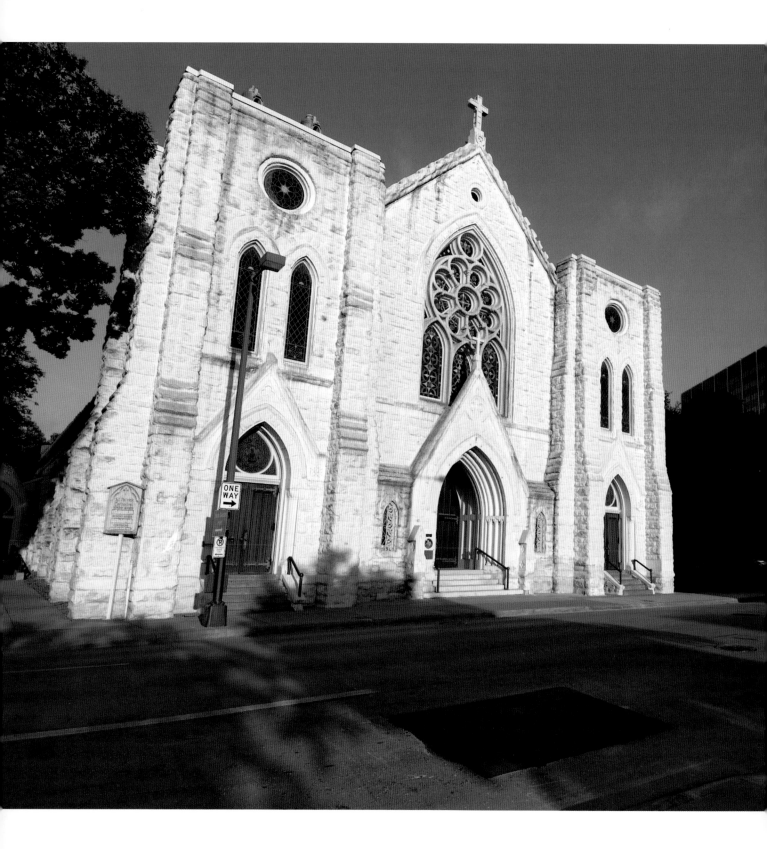

St. Patrick's Cathedral

This historic, stone cathedral was designed in the popular Gothic Revival style with twin towers topped by lofty towers, however, the towers were never built. The church is magnificently detailed with a large stained-glass rose above the main entrance and pointed arches with leaded glass on other windows and entry ways. Today, this downtown church serves a congregation of 4,000.

ENTERED IN
THE NATIONAL REGISTER
OF HISTORIC PLACES
1985

STATE HISTORICAL SURVEY COMMITTEE

TEXAS

ST. PATRICK'S CATHEDRAL
ERECTED 1888-1892 UNDER THE
DIRECTION OF THE PARISH PRIEST,
THE REV. JEAN M. GUYOT, A NATIVE
OF FRANCE. STONE FOR WALLS WAS
QUARRIED LOCALLY. IMPROVISED,
HORSE-POWERED LATHES WERE USED
TO TURN AND POLISH THE EIGHTEEN
INTERIOR PILLARS. CEILINGS AND
WINDOW FRAMES ARE WOOD GRAINED.
STAINED GLASS WINDOWS WERE
IMPORTED FROM MUNICH, GERMANY.
BELL, CAST IN TROY, NEW YORK, HAS
BEEN IN USE SINCE 1888.
RECORDED TEXAS HISTORIC LANDMARK—1962

Historic Texas Landmark

The stunning St. Patrick's Cathedral was
built in 1888 and is the oldest, continuously
used church building in Fort Worth. It is
largely intact architecturally and has recent-
ly gone through several years of restoration.

M. E. Sadler Hall (*top and bottom*)

Built in 1959, M. E. Sadler Hall serves as Texas Christian University's administration building. It is an outstanding example of the work of distinguished architects, Sanguinet and Staats, designers of many of Fort Worth's significant buildings. The University has nearly nine-thousand students enrolled in seven schools and colleges, including humanities, divinity, business, fine arts, communications, and science and engineering.

Texas Christian University

Texas Christian University was founded in 1873 as a frontier school named AddRan College in Waco, Texas. It was recognized as Texas Christian University in 1902. When a fire destroyed its main building eight years later, the city of Forth Worth offered the university fifty acres of land and $200,000 to rebuild their campus in Fort Worth. The university accepted the city's offer, and the present campus continues to grow and prosper in southwest Fort Worth.

Japanese Garden Serenity

The beautiful Japanese Garden at Fort Worth Botanic Gardens is a sanctuary for the senses. In 1970, Fort Worth's sister city, Nagaoka, Japan, donated many plants and materials to create garden features that include a teahouse, Zen meditation garden, pagoda, and moon-viewing deck.

DEBORAH BEGGS MONCRIEF GARDEN CENTER

BOTANIC GARDEN CENTER

Fort Worth Botanic Gardens

The oldest in Texas, the Botanic Gardens create a flowing landscape of magnificent shade trees, flowering shrubs, and native and exotic plants punctuated with waterfalls, ponds, reflecting pools and whimsical sculptures such as this leaping frog at the Gardens' entrance.

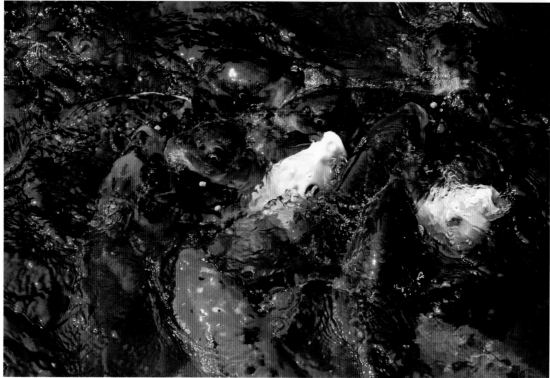

Japanese Garden Pavilion (*top*)

The pavilion area of the Japanese Garden is the setting for seasonal festivals including the annual spring *Butterflies in the Garden*. Thousands of butterflies take flight creating a spectacular display.

Koi Pond (*bottom*)

Ponds throughout the Japanese Garden are filled with brightly colored koi, a popular variety of the common carp fish developed by Japanese breeders. Koi have become increasingly popular in American water gardens.

Zen Garden (*opposite*)

Used historically by Zen Buddhists as a focus for meditation, a Zen garden contains carefully positioned stones that represent tranquil islands in a sea that seems to ripple with the thoughtful strokes of finely raked sand.

Tarrant County Courthouse (*above*)

This magnificent Beaux Arts courthouse sits high on a bluff overlooking the Trinity River. At a height of 194 feet, a copper dome crowns the 1895 structure. Short of its hundredth birthday, the grand building was painstakingly renovated to reflect its original beauty.

Duty **Memorial** (*opposite*)

Veterans Memorial Park is dedicated to those who served at Fort Worth's Camp Bowie and to veterans of all wars. The *Duty* memorial statue honors American soldiers who gave their lives liberating Belgium during World War I.

DUTY
DEDICATED
TO THE MEMORY OF ALL VETERANS
BY
VETERANS OF WORLD WAR I U.S.A
THE DEPARTMENT OF

IN FLANDERS FIELDS

IN FLANDERS FIELDS THE POPPIES BLOW
BETWEEN THE CROSSES ROW ON ROW
THAT MARK OUR PLACE AND IN THE SKY
THE LARKS, STILL BRAVELY SINGING FLY
SCARCE HEARD AMID THE GUNS BELOW
WE ARE THE DEAD SHORT DAYS AGO WE LIVED
FELT DAWN SAW SUNSET GLOW
LOVED AND WERE LOVED AND NOW WE LIE

Nancy Lee and Perry R. Bass Performance Hall (top)

Home to the Fort Worth Symphony Orchestra, the Texas Ballet Theater, and the Fort Worth Opera, this highly acclaimed performance venue has been dubbed "one of the top ten opera houses in the world" by *Travel and Leisure Magazine*.

Trumpeting Angel (bottom)

Flanking the entrance of the performance hall, two 48-foot-tall angels herald a greeting to arriving guests. These graceful, limestone statues, carved by Marton Varo, have come to symbolize the rich, cultural treasures of the Fort Worth-Dallas metropolitan area.

Opening Night (opposite)

Over 2,000 people can be seated for performances beneath the hand-painted Great Dome at the Founders Concert Theater. Fort Worth has the third largest cultural district in America.

Geodesic Dome

Inspired by the innovative designs of R. Buckminster Fuller, architect Henry Kaiser created the stunning, geodesic-domed Casa Mañana Theatre, the first permanent theater in America designed for musicals-in-the-round.

Casa Mañana Theatre

Casa Mañana is the largest performing arts organization in North Texas and has entertained audiences for forty years with an exciting repertoire of dramas, comedies, concerts, Broadway musicals, and touring shows.

Rose Marine Theater

Opened in 1918 as a movie house, this historic theater began showing movies in Spanish in the 1940s. Today, the theater hosts public events, as well as live performances of the Latin Arts Association, Fort Worth's only Hispanic theater company.

Fort Worth Public Library

The main branch of the public library started out completely underground in 1978, with Lamar Street traffic rumbling above. When the roof began leaking, this beautiful two-story addition was added.

Kimbell Art Museum *(top and bottom)*

The Kimbell Art Museum opened to rave reviews in 1972, thanks in great part to the award-winning architecture of Louis I. Khan. Of his design, Khan said, *"The building feels…that I have nothing to do with it…that some other hand did it."* From the works of Caravaggio to Monet to Mondrian and contemporaries, Kimbell has many treasures, including an impressive collection of Asian art. It has a well-earned reputation as America's best small museum.

Art in Design

One of America's great buildings, Kimbell Art Museum's design consists of a connected series of long, barrel-vaulted exhibit halls that incorporate natural light. In this intimate setting, visitors experience the full impact and subtleties of the artist's brush or the sculptor's tools.

Floating Islands of Art (*pages 36–37*)

The flat-roofed pavilions of the new Modern Art Museum of Fort Worth rise dramatically out of a shimmering pond. This profound design, by Japanese architect Tadao Ando, reflects the clean, unadorned elements of modern art itself.

Modern Art Museum of Fort Worth (*above*)

Chartered in 1892, "The Modern" is one of the oldest museums in the western United States. Dedicated to postwar art, its impressive collection includes 2,600 paintings, sculptures, drawings, prints, photographs, videotapes, and slides.

Vortex (*opposite*)

Soaring high above the museum's roofline is a massive, 230-ton sculpture by Richard Serra. *Vortex* was manufactured in Germany, the only place in the world that could handle the immense sheets of steel.

Fort Worth Nature and Science Museum

The Lone Star Dinosaur exhibit at the Fort Worth Nature and Science Museum is an ever-changing display, thanks to the field work of the paleontologists on staff. For the past seventeen years, the museum has joined forces with the faculty at Southern Methodist University to conduct regional digs. Together they have uncovered exciting finds of dinosaur bones and fossils and are responsible for identifying five new species.

Prehistoric Worlds (*top*)

Dino Dig is a popular interactive exhibit where children become paleontologists and dig for dinosaur bones. The oldest children's museum in Texas, this noted facility has an IMAX Dome theater, a planetarium, and hundreds of fun exhibits.

Knee High to a Dinosaur (*bottom*)

One average size human is barely as tall as the knee joint of a gigantic Cretaceous dinosaur that once roamed an ancient sea near present-day Fort Worth. The Lone Star Dinosaur exhibit always thrills visitors with the latest, prehistoric finds.

Bureau of Engraving and Printing

The Visitors' Center at the Bureau of Engraving and Printing offers guided tours of the money-making process with special demonstrations of antique printing presses, an engraver's bench, and what becomes of mutilated bills that are taken out of circulation.

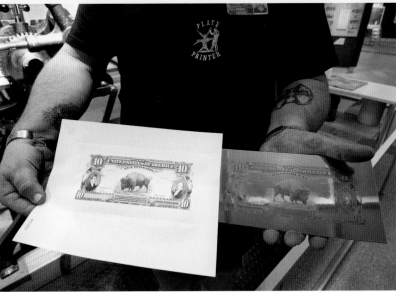

Visitors' Center Exhibits (*top*)

Two floors of interactive exhibits show the history of currency and the complex process of printing money. By the end of the tour, you may want to become a *notaphilist*– a collector of paper money.

Commemorative Bill (*bottom, left*)

A press operator shows a commemorative ten-dollar bill during a special printing demonstration on an antique spider press. Tourists learn fascinating facts about the money-making process on this popular tour.

Hot Off the Presses (*bottom, right*)

During a tour of the Western Currency Facility, the process of printing billions of dollars can be viewed from an enclosed walkway above the money-making machines.

Cattle Baron Lifestyle (*above*)

This historic, 18-room mansion was built in 1903 during the golden era of the cattle barons. A rare example of Georgian Revival architecture in the southwest, the mansion is restored with many original furnishings.

Historic Quality Hill (*opposite, top*)

At the turn of the 20th century, The Ball-Eddleman-McFarland House was built in an exclusive neighborhood of wealthy cattle barons. It is Fort Worth's most outstanding example of the Queen Anne Victorian style. ·

Ball-Eddleman-McFarland House (*opposite, bottom*)

The house is a rare treasure in Fort Worth because many of this type did not survive the passage of time. It is also unique because only three families have lived here over several decades, and the original design was barely altered.

19th-Century Craftsmanship (*left and right*)

The exquisite craftsmanship of the Ball-Eddleman-McFarland House reflects the spectacular features of the Queen Anne-style. Elaborate oak and mahogany wood-work details every room, including this entrance foyer staircase and wainscoting.

The hardwood floors feature an elegant maple-leaf pattern with contrasting light and dark in-laid woods. Every surface of this house offers a unique opportunity for artistry.

Fine Dining (*opposite*)

Period furnishings enhance the rich patterns of woodworking on the ceiling, walls and floors of this elegant dining room. A built-in corner hutch displays silverware and glassware used by prominent Fort Worth families.

Confederate Colors (*top*)

The Texas Civil War Museum shows its colors with over sixty carefully preserved flags, many of which were flown in Texas regiments that fought for the Confederacy. The flag collection, alone, is valued at $3 million.

Period Style (*bottom*)

A variety of Civil War uniforms and firearms are on display at the Texas Civil War Museum. In addition to the military clothing, there is wonderful collection of textiles and clothing, including over two-hundred Victorian-era dresses.

Texas Civil War Museum

Opened in 2006, this new Fort Worth museum brings together one of the largest private collections of Civil War artifacts in North America and the collection of the Texas Division of the United Daughters of the Confederacy.

Buffalo Soldiers (*opposite*)

The National Cowboys of Color Museum and Hall of Fame pays tribute to the bravery of the famous Buffalo Soldiers units which were comprised of African Americans. Other exhibits honor Hispanics, European and Native-Americans' efforts.

Flying Saucer Draught Emporium (*top*)

Conveniently located in Sundance Square, downtown Fort Worth's shopping and entertainment center, Flying Saucer is a favorite with beer lovers. Over one-hundred beers are on tap, and the atmosphere is pure fun.

Bikers in Sundance Square (*bottom*)

Good food and live music are served up regularly at 8.0 in Sundance Square, a fun place to enjoy with a date or to meet with a group of motorcycle buddies. The square has something for everyone's taste.

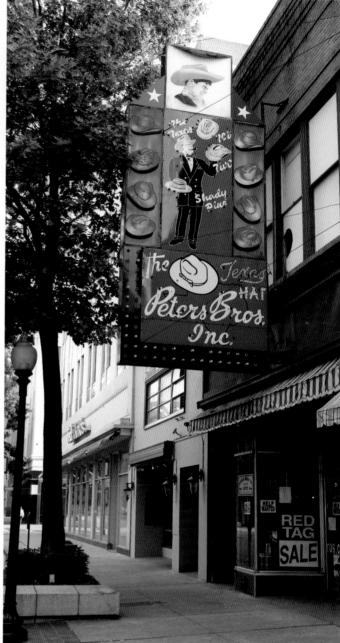

Music at The Ranch (*left*)

Fort Worth's favorite country-western music station is The Ranch, broadcasting great county tunes from Sundance Square. The Ranch is "The Sound of Fort Worth".

Peters Brothers Hats (*right*)

In business for nearly 100 years, Peters Brothers' custom-made hats became famous when Fort Worth promoter and philanthropist Amon Carter began giving them as gifts to celebrities.

Haltom's Jewelers Clock (*opposite*)

When historic Fort Worth retailer Haltom's Jewelers agreed to relocate to Sundance Square, their famous street clock had to go with them. Now the clock keeps time on the corner of Third and Main.

Sundance Stroll (*pages 54–55*)

At dusk, Sundance Square beckons people to stroll through this hip entertainment district. They can pick their pleasures from boutiques, shops, galleries, restaurants, hotels, and clubs.

Reata at Sundance Square (*opposite*)

Reata stands tall in Sundance Square with four floors of festivities. Top-notch chefs prepare legendary Western cuisine with a cosmopolitan twist, while two trendy bars and a rooftop view of the downtown lights make for a perfect evening.

Chisholm Trail Mural (*top and bottom*)

Created by trompe l'oeil artist Richard Haas, this mural celebrates Fort Worth's historical role as a cattle town on the Chisholm Trail which stretched from San Antonio to the beef markets in Kansas. The mural is located on the side of the historic Jett Building in Sundance Square.

White Elephant Saloon (*opposite*)

An authentic, wild west saloon in the Historic Stockyards District, White Elephant is one of the best 100 bars in America and lives up to its fame with live C&W music, dancing, and a huge collection of cowboy hats and elephants.

Billy Bob's Texas (*top and bottom*)

Opened in 1981, Billy Bob's quickly set a new record as the largest honky-tonk in the world. Live C&W bands and a big dance floor make it hard to resist grabbing your partner and doing the Texas two-step. This world-famous club covers three acres with dozens of bar stations, a restaurant, arcade games, a "Wall of Fame" with celebrity handprints, a general store, and its own indoor rodeo arena for professional bull riding.

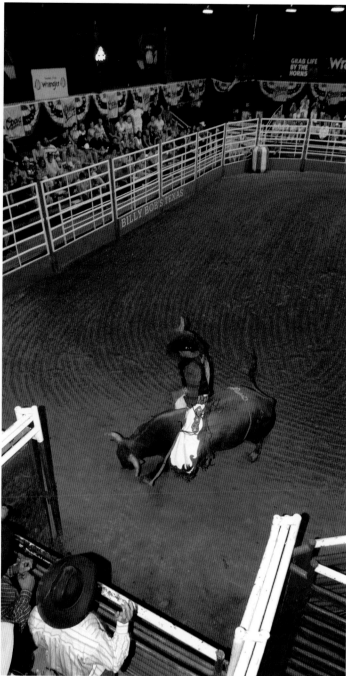

World's Largest "Honky-Tonk" (*left*)

Billy Bob's building has seen a lot of action since 1910. It was an open-air cattle barn, a World War II airplane factory, and a department store. Its twenty-acre parking lot accommodates large crowds for big-name C&W shows.

Ride 'em Cowboy (*right*)

The action is always hot at Billy Bob's, but it's even wilder on Friday and Saturday nights in the honky-tonk's own rodeo arena. Cowboys face formidable challengers as they put on a fantastic show.

Billiards at Billy Bob's

Whether it's a game of eight ball or a Willie
Nelson concert, Billy Bob's has the kind of
entertainment that always draws a crowd.
Over fifteen million people have spent a
memorable day or night here since this
honky-tonk opened in 1981.

Calf Roping at Cowtown

Each weekend, Stockyards Championship Rodeo comes to Cowtown Coliseum, thrilling crowds with calf roping, bull riding, team roping, barrel racing and other exciting, edge-of-your-seat thrills.

Bucking Bronco

Every second is an eternity while hanging onto the back of a bucking bronco, but these cowboys know how to take the fall, brush themselves off, and get ready for the next event.

Ready to Ride (*top*)

A spirited bronco almost jumps the gate, while cowboys attempt to bring him back into the stall, just one example of the many surprises during a typical night at Stockyards Championship Rodeo.

Stockyards Championship Rodeo (*bottom*)

Bull riding as a rodeo event was introduced at Cowtown Coliseum in 1934 before eager crowds. Riders must stay on the bull for a full eight seconds to stay in the competition. Often, the bull doesn't cooperate.

Out of the Gate

Rodeo history has been made time and time again in the hallowed arena of Cowtown Coliseum. It was the site of the world's first indoor rodeo in 1918 and the world's first live radio broadcast of a rodeo in 1923. It was also the setting of historic non-rodeo appearances by Comanche braves, two American presidents, famed opera singer Enrico Caruso, Elvis Presley, the Russian Ballet, Bob Hope and Doris Day.

Signage with a Kick (*left*)

Signage featuring a unique neon boot with an art deco flair, marks one of Fort Worth's most prestigious and historic businesses. In addition to a fantastic ready-made selection of fine western clothing, Leddy's also provides custom saddles and boots.

A Texas Legend (*right and opposite*)

M. L. Leddy's Boots and Saddlery boasts four-generations of expert leather craftsmenship. These experienced artisans custom-make each boot and saddle from start to finish using top-grade materials. The exceptional beauty and quality of their work has made Leddy's world-famous.

Cowboy Chic *(above and opposite)*

M. L. Leddy's Boots and Saddlery sells a variety of western styles from ranch-hand tough to sizzling styles for red-carpet celebrities. In its high-end boutique, you'll find the couture creations of designers such as Ermenegildo Zegna, pure beaver cowboy hats, emerald-studded belt buckles and boots made of chartreuse lizard and purple stingray. A separate room features the real-cowboy hard tackle, the works you need to run a ranch.

Beaumont Ranch at Grandview (*above*)

One of the best dude ranches in Texas is just thirty-five miles from Fort Worth. Beaumont is a working cattle ranch with a 40,000- acre spread and its own 1880's western town, Chisholm Fork. It's great for a romantic getaway, a western-style wedding, a family vacation or a corporate team-building retreat. As the staff will say, *"Just tell us what part of the Old West you want to experience, and we'll do our best to deliver it."*

Leather, Lines, and Hands (*opposite*)

The hands of this Beaumont ranch cowboy were photographed just before heading off to work the cattle.

70

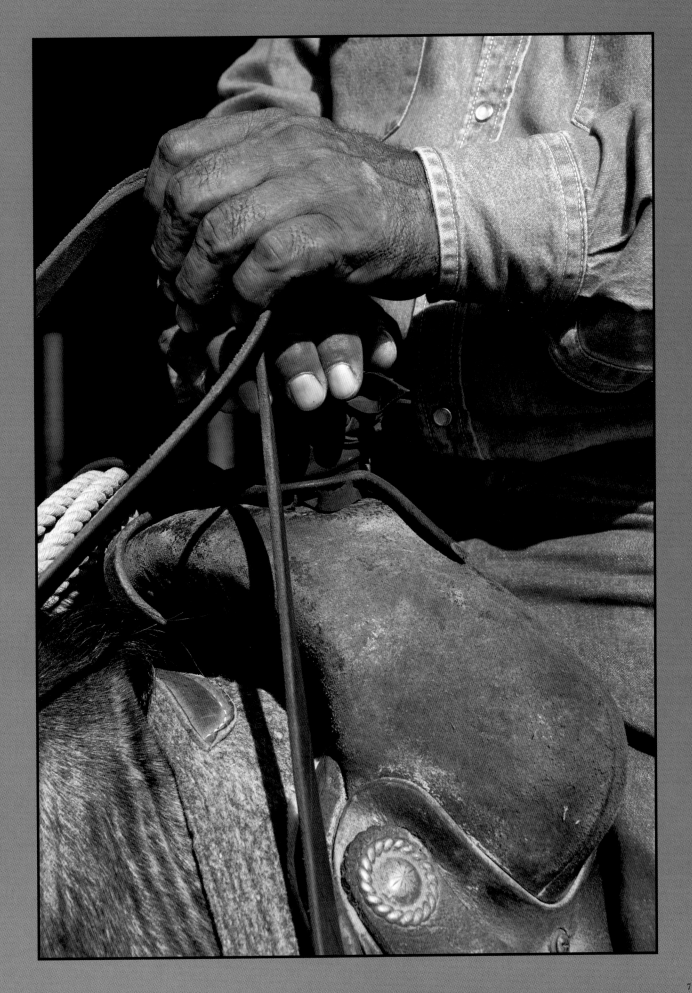

Beaumont Cowboys

Beaumont ranch hands are hardworking and friendly. From branding to bird watching, the ranch offers many activities that allow visitors to create their own personalized adventure.

Western Style

The tack room at the Beaumont Ranch is
well-stocked and ready for riders. The
ranch offers great trail rides and more,
such as picnics, fishing, ranch rodeos and
authentic chuck wagon breakfasts.

Gun Fights at Chisholm Fork

Beaumont Ranch's own little Wild West town is a great setting for living history events, such as gun fights, cattle drives and exhibitions of the Seventh Calvary reenactments.

Chisholm Trail

The historic Chisholm Trail stretched from San Antonio to several Kansas towns, at different times, and ran right through the middle of Beaumont Ranch. Today, visitors can celebrate this historic trail by signing up for the ranch's "Cowboy Up" cattle drive which includes lots of time in the saddle, plus sharp shooting practice with real six shooters, relay roping, cutting cattle competition, a hot pepper eating contest, a Texas cookout and a special "Cowboy Idol" competition.

Log Cabin Village (*opposite*)

A stylish scarecrow wards off birds in an herb garden of an authentic 19th-century log cabin. Inside and out, interpreters demonstrate vital skills that Texan pioneers needed to survive, including weaving and knitting, candle making, corn milling and nail making.

Pickard Cabin (*above*)

One of the Village's eight restored log homes, Pickard Cabin, features period furniture and period performers dressed in 19th-century costume. Visitors can watch them weave on a shot loom just like in frontier days.

Shaw Cabin and Gristmill

This 1854 cabin showcases the impressive craftsmanship of a master builder of frontier log homes. Tom Shaw was well-known for his carpentry skills and helped many other homesteaders build their log homes. The 19th-century working grist mill was added in 1970 and has produced ready-to-use corn meal since then. Relocated to the Log Cabin Village, the house was originally in an extreme frontier area of Texas.

Living History

Stroll down the lanes of this quaint village of log cabins in Fort Worth's Forest Park, and step back in time to the Texas frontier. The village staff lovingly recreates different tools and skills required in 19th-century daily life.

Texas and Southwest Cattle Raiser's
Museum *(top and bottom)*

Dioramas, artifacts and interactive exhibits
set the stage for the lively history of the
Texas frontier from the perspective of cattle
barons, cowboys, ranchers, ranch hands
and rustlers. Authentic artifacts include the
world's largest documented branding iron

collection with brands used by Nolan Ryan,
Stephen F. Austin, and the King Ranch.
The Ken Spain Saddle Collection and the
Joe Russell Spur Collection are favorites
as well.

Texas Rangers

The Texas and Southwest Cattle Raisers Museum features an exhibit on the legendary Texas Rangers who were appointed by the Texas and Southwest Cattle Raisers Association to catch cattle rustlers. These specially commissioned inspectors proved to be invaluable as they combined legal authority with detective skills and knowledge of the cattle industry. In 2002 alone, the Texas Rangers helped recover over $4 million worth of livestock and property.

National Cowgirl Museum and Hall of Fame (*top*)

This Fort Worth museum documents the lives of women and their contributions to the American West from the mid-1800s to the present. Over 5,000 artifacts and 2,500 photographs tell many inspiring stories of courageous women.

Saddle Up (*bottom*)

Hand-carved panels on the museum's façade depict thematic scenes, including that of a young cowgirl getting ready to ride. Richard Haas' trompe l'oeil mural on the side of the building is of five cowgirls seemingly riding at full gallop out of the building.

High Desert Princess (*opposite*)

Sculptor Mehl Lawson captures the strength and independence of the Texan cowgirl, and cowgirls everywhere, in an exquisite life-size, bronze sculpture that graces the lawn of the Cowgirl Museum.

Hall of Fame (*above*)

The women inducted into the National Cowgirl Hall of Fame were pioneers, entertainers, artists, writers, tribal leaders, suffragettes, modern ranchers and rodeo cowgirls—each making their mark as part of a great American legacy.

Sacagawea (*opposite*)

A Shoshone Indian woman, Sacagawea was the famous interpreter and guide for the Lewis and Clark expedition into the newly acquired Louisiana Purchase Territories. She helped secure safe passage through treacherous terrain.

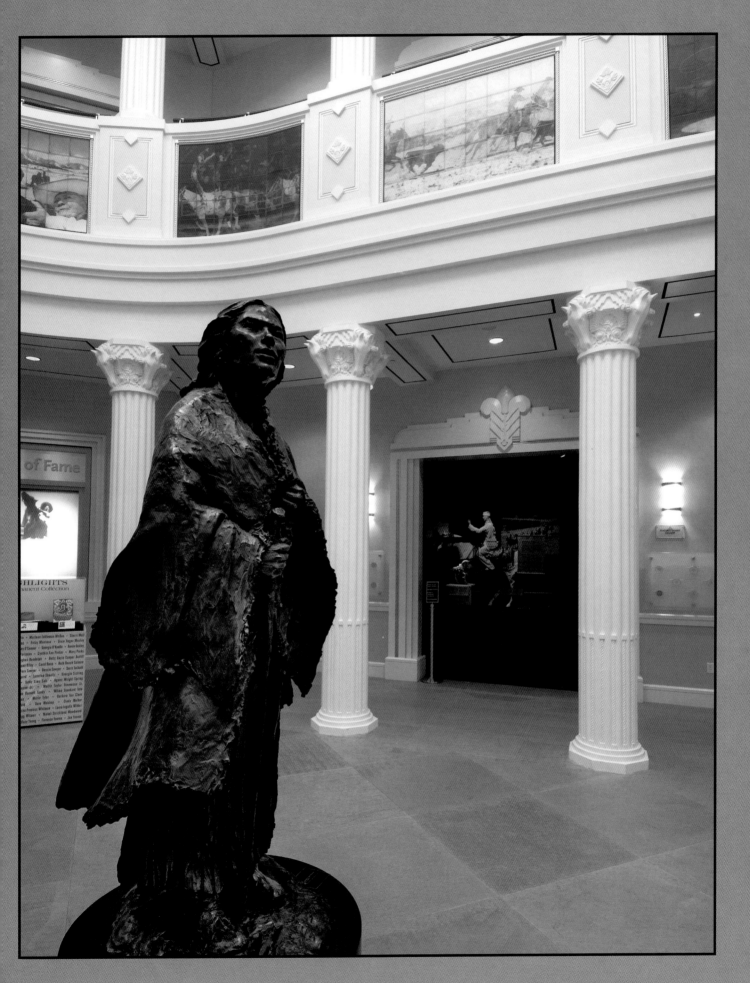

Texas Cowboy Hall of Fame (*opposite*)

The new Texas Cowboy Hall of Fame has set up house in an old barn at the Stockyards that once housed horses and mules. It pays tribute to Texas' top cowboys and cowgirls with photographs and memorabilia of their lives.

Sterquell Wagon Collection (*top*)

Hungry cowboys gather around a campfire next to the chuck wagon in one of the exhibits of the world's largest lifestyle wagon collections. The exhibit features more than sixty antique wagons, carriages and sleighs.

Period Portraiture (*bottom*)

A well-dressed woman poses for her photograph in front of a camera on a tripod. The exhibit features an antique wagon that once belonged to Levi Hand, a landscape and portrait photographer from New Jersey in the early 1900's.

Texas and Pacific Railway Office
Building (*opposite and above*)

An outstanding example of the 1920's
Zigzag Moderne architecture, this twelve-
story structure was part of the massive
downtown complex built by Texas and
Pacific Railroad, which also included a
warehouse and terminal. The elaborate
details of the lobby are uncovered, thanks
to a recent renovation. Like many of the
city's grand, historic buildings, this old
office building is being converted into
residential space.

Intermodal Transportation Center

Striking clay murals adorn the walls of the
new Intermodal Transportation Center in
downtown Fort Worth. Five murals framed
in a long, brick wall set the stage for these
scenes from the neighborhood's past.

History in Clay (*top and bottom*)

Murals by artist Paula Blincoe Collins depict the lifestyle and history of the area's African-American businesses from post-Civil War to 1940. The rough-hewed style enhances its historical perspective. The transportation center was designed to blend the city's past with the newer downtown landscape. A special salute to the past, the building's four-faced clock tower rises seven stories, helping to keep this busy city on time.

Will Rogers Memorial Center

(above and opposite)

The Will Rogers Memorial Center hosts every event from rodeos to rock and roll. Its art deco tile mural at the top lights up at sunset. An impressive statue of Will Rogers on his beloved horse, Soapsuds, pays tribute to this American icon who was a hero to all who aspired to be a cowboy. Part Cherokee, Will Rogers once remarked about his heritage as an American: *"My folks didn't come over on the Mayflower, but a few met the boat."*

Cowtown Coliseum

Historic Cowtown Coliseum was built in
1907 as the "largest and most elegant livestock exhibition building in America." It
is now synonymous with great rodeos and
Pawnee Bill's Wild West Show, a recreation
of the original one from 1909.

Fort Worth Stockyards

In Fort Worth's heyday as a booming cattle town, it took a strong latch to keep the gates securely closed when the cattle pens were filled with Texas long-horn steer. Each had an average weight of 1800 to 2000 pounds.

Cattle Pens

Cattle pens at the Historic Fort Worth Stockyards are quiet testimony to the exciting era when the Wild West was booming. Once the railroad came to town, Fort Worth exploded with growth.

Stockyard Blooms

The history of this old cattle town is kept alive today in this national historic district, the site of the only daily cattle drive in America. Visitors can watch real drovers herd real cattle at Stockyards Station.

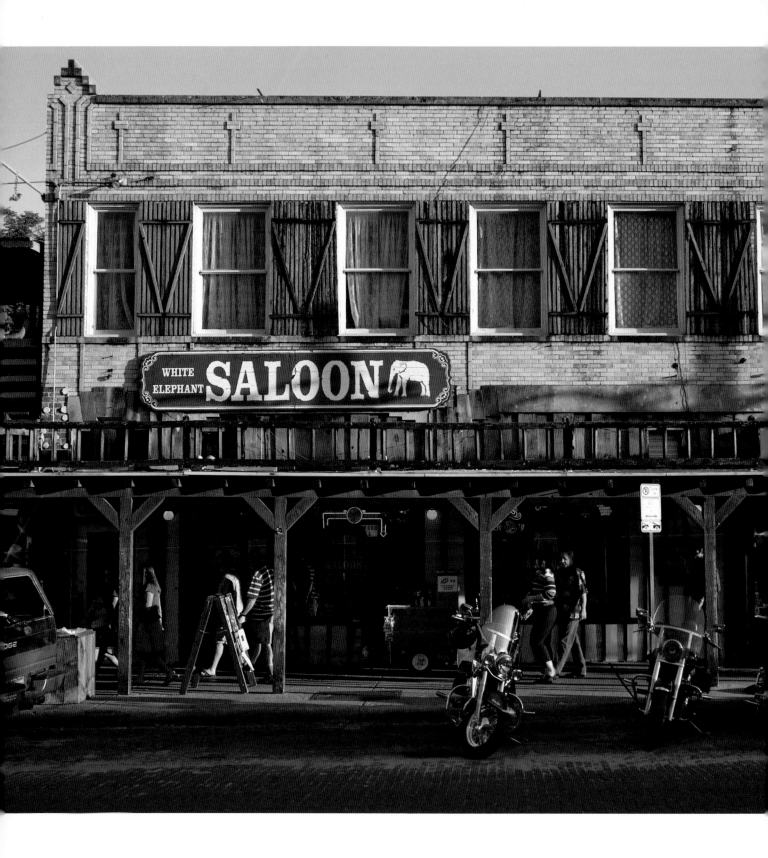

White Elephant Saloon

The epitome of a great, western saloon, this
100-year-old watering hole provides a
glimpse of the Wild West's past. Every year
on February 8th, the White Elephant stages
an historical reenactment of the last gun-
fight in Fort Worth that occured in front of
this famous saloon.

The Cross Eyed Moose

The Cross Eyed Moose is a chic, Western boutique with fine, one-of-a-kind western furniture, well-suited for cattle barons and oil tycoons. Unique accent pieces round out these upscale finds.

Puffy the Steam Train (*above*)

When the vintage steam train, Puffy, arrives at Stockyards Station from Grapevine, twenty-one miles away, the engine reverses direction on a turnabout to take passengers south for a ten-mile trek along the famous Chisholm Trail.

Stockyards Station (*opposite*)

Stockyards Station features modern shops with 19th-century storefronts, filled with everything Western. Other attractions include galleries, museums, and a ride on the Tarantula Train, the only operational steam train in Texas.

THE OLD CHISHOLM TRAIL

THIS TRAIL POST COMMEMORATES AND
MARKS THE LOCATION OF THE GREAT
EASTERN CATTLE ROAD, KNOWN COMMONLY
AS THE OLD CHISHOLM TRAIL, AS IT LEFT FT.
WORTH AND HEADED NORTH TOWARD RED
RIVER STATION AND INDIAN TERRITORY. IT IS
IDENTICAL TO 400 CHISHOLM TRAIL POSTS
PLACED ACROSS OKLAHOMA (INDIAN
TERRITORY) FROM 1990 TO 1997 BY ROBERT
L. (BOB) KLEMME OF ENID, OK, TO MARK THE
EXACT TRAIL FROM RED RIVER STATION TO
KANSAS, SET DURING THE CHISHOLM TRAIL
ROUNDUP, 16 JUNE, 2000.

(COURTESY OF ROBERT L. (BOB) KLEMME
ENID, OK, AND THE CHISHOLM TRAIL
HERITAGE CENTER, DUNCAN, OK.)

Chisholm Trail Marker (*above*)

After the Civil War, cattle drives from
South Texas passed through Fort Worth on
their way to Abilene, Wichita and other
Central Kansas beef markets. When the
railroad arrived and stock yards were built,
Fort Worth boomed.

Bill Pickett (*opposite*)

A former slave, Bill Pickett became the
most famous African-American rodeo
performer in history. The sculpture at
Cowtown Coliseum depicts him wrestling
a steer, a rodeo event he invented in 1903.

RED & CHARLINE MCCOMBS
SOUTHWEST SUPPLY COMPANY
GARY HAVARD
GEORGE & LISA PERRY
CHRIS SCHARBAUER
PERRY R. BASS
CAROL VANHORNE BECKER
PATTI & BILLY BOB BARNETT
FRANK D. KENT
WILL G

The Stockyards Museum

At the museum in the historic Livestock
Exchange Building, cast iron skillets and
other heavy household items are a testa-
ment to Western American lifestyle during
a more rugged era.

The Mountain Man

Renowned Amercian artist Frederic Remington created an incredibly detailed bronze sculpture in 1912 to honor a vanished breed of frontiersmen. Full-size replicas, such as this, are sold by Fort Worth retailer Cross-Eyed Moose.

Head First (*above*)

In addition to its fantastic cowboy and
cowgirl museums and historic preservation
areas, Forth Worth celebrates its Cowtown
heritage on every possible public surface,
like the side of this building near the
Stockyards.

Stockyards Hotel (*opposite*)

This historic 1907 Texas landmark lodged
cattle barons and their families, cowboys,
businessmen and foreign dignitaries. Today
guests can choose from Victorian, Cowboy,
Mountain Man, and Native American-
themed rooms.

History in Bloom

Banks of flowers bloom on the grounds
of the historic Fort Worth Livestock
Exchange. Today it houses the museum of
the North Fort Worth Historical Society
and headquarters of Lone Star Airlines.

Fort Worth Livestock Exchange

In 1902 this large, adobe-style building was erected as a center for cattle traders. It soon became known as "the Wall Street of the West." Livestock prices around the world were posted here. The Exchange housed a bank, post office, five railroad offices and three telegraph offices. Always bustling with activity, it was the nerve center of a massive system that traded as many as five million animals per year—cattle, sheep, hogs, horses and mules.

The Wedding Chapel

Young flower girls in fancy gowns with
ribbons in their hair get their instructions
before they walk down the aisle at this little
wedding chapel and photography studio at
Stockyard Station.

Old Time Music

Musicians strumming guitars and fiddles
bring back that old time music for tourists
as they browse the unique shops, galleries
and food concessions at Stockyard Station.

Chuckie

Manufactured by Boeing, Chuckie, the legendary B-17 Flying Fortress at Fort Worth's Vintage Flying Museum, made history in the air during World War II with its unrelenting, strategic bombing missions of German industrial targets. These bombers were flown by the Eighth Air Force Squadron in England and the Fifteenth Squadron in Italy. Built in 1944, Chuckie is unique because it still flies and participates in air shows.

Vintage Flying Museum

Fort Worth's Vintage Flying Museum features an array of vintage aircraft such as wartime trainers, bi-planes, and home-made tri-planes. It is an impressive collection of aviation history.

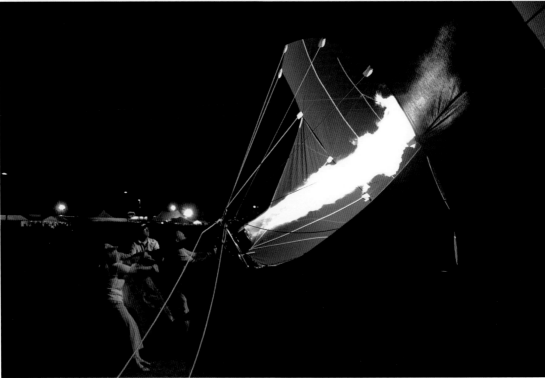

Plano Balloon Festival (*top and opposite*)

Every September, for three days, the skies over Plano, Texas are filled with colorful hot air balloons. The festival attracts over 100,000 visitors who come to watch seventy-five balloons take flight. On the ground, visitors enjoy live bands, festivities and funnel cakes, a festival favorite.

All Fired Up (*bottom*)

When the sun goes down, the Plano Balloon Festival shifts into another gear. Nighttime balloon flights create their own spectacle, as if dozens of bonfires suddenly rise together into the dark, star-studded skies.

The Richard Petty Driving Experience
(above, below, and opposite)

The Richard Petty Driving Experience is one of several driving schools at the Texas Motor Speedway. The schools plan their classes between major races, and there is seldom an empty seat. Racing fans from all walks of life sign up to experience the thrill of driving a race car at speeds up to 150 miles per hour. The Petty Experience is a highly acclaimed motor sports entertainment company and provides an exciting once-in-a-lifetime thrill for aspiring race car drivers.

Texas Motor Speedway (*top*)

The Texas Motor Speedway's 1.5-mile track is shaped in a quad-oval design, very similar to the speedways in Atlanta and Charlotte. Qualifying rounds on the NASCAR circuit in 2004 and 2005 made it the fastest track of its type.

Stremme Power (*bottom*)

David Stremme, 2002 Rookie of the Year, became the first Busch Series driver in 2003 to take top rookie honors even though he didn't compete in the full season. In 2006, he placed in the top 20 four times, his best ever.

Need for Speed

Racing fans all over the world can easily identify this No. 43 Cheerios/Betty Crocker Dodge, one of the cars driven by Richard Petty's powerhouse racing team. Petty made racing history as a seven-time NASCAR champion.

Famous Chicken

In 2005, the Fort Worth Cats had their
mojo working as they won the minor league
championship again, for the first time since
1948, and repeated their lucky streak in
2006. "Famous Chicken" travels from ballpark to ballpark putting on his show. He
got his start as "The San Diego Chicken."

Fort Worth Cats

The Cats, Fort Worth's minor league base-ball team, was a founding member of the Texas League in 1888, with many winning seasons and several championship years. Today's modern facility was built in 2001 on top of the old 1926 stadium, with home plate remaining in the exact same place.

Baseball Fever (*top and bottom*)

Named one of the top 10 independent parks in the nation by Baseball America, the new La Grave Field stadium represents a return of minor league baseball to Fort Worth for the first time since 1964. Leading this exciting renaissance is the Cats' new owner Carl Bell, who grew up watching games on the old La Grave baseball diamond. Enthusiastic fans can look forward to cheering their team in forty-eight home games next season.

Cats Hero

Signed by the Cats in 2006, pitcher Danny Valentin gives autographs for eager, young fans after a home game at La Grave Stadium. He came from back-to-back 10-win seasons for Edinburg in the Central League in 2003 and 2004.

Fort Worth Zoo (*above and opposite*)

Fort Worth Zoo is one of four American zoos that has successfully bred lions—two were born in 2004 and a litter of four made headlines in 2005. The nationally ranked zoo supports over twenty conservation projects around the world. After some hard times and successful private fundraising, the Fort Worth Zoo held a grand re-opening in 1992 and introduced two, new habitats, World of Primates and Asian Falls. Annual zoo attendance soared to one million visitors. Every year, the number of visitors continues to rise as the zoo takes its place as one of the country's top zoos.

Turtles and Much More

Turtles, elephants, tigers, gorillas, giraffes, snakes, parrots, lions, antelopes, meerkats, and predatory birds—the Fort Worth Zoo exhibits 435 species in total. This award-winning zoo distinguishes itself with comprehensive exhibits of all four Great Apes species, three of five rhino species, one of the country's largest reptile collections, and one of only four zoos with active breeding programs for Asian elephants and African lions.

Maternal Instinct

A flamingo nuzzles its egg in poignant
symbolism of the cycle of life, fertility and
birth at this nationally acclaimed zoo. The
Fort Worth Zoo has come a long way since
it was founded in 1909 with 10 animals.
It is the oldest continuous zoo site in the
state of Texas.

Photograph by Ana Rosa Calvin

Peter A. Calvin

Peter A. Calvin studied photography at the Butler Institute of American Art, Ohio University (BFA), and Texas A&M University –Commerce (MFA). After spending several years in Mexico in the late 1980's, he returned to Dallas, where he lives with his wife, Ana Rosa, and their son, Peter Jose.

In addition to his personal work, Peter shoots for selected editorial and commercial clients, and is an Ad Interim Instructor of Art in the photography program at Texas A&M University–Commerce. His work has been published in Europe, Canada, Mexico, and the United States. His fine art work is represented by the Afterimage Gallery in Dallas, Texas.